BLACK SQUARE EDITIONS

NEW YORK   2003

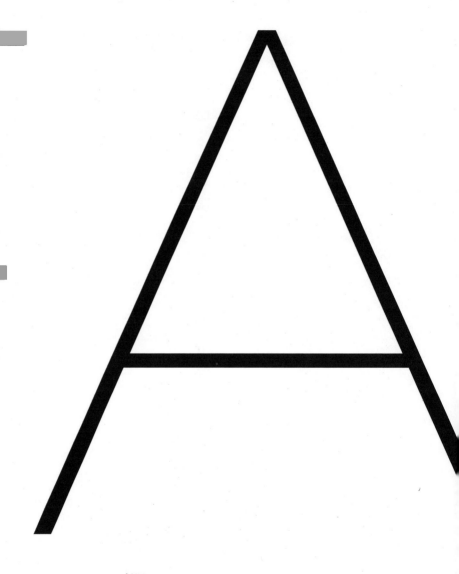

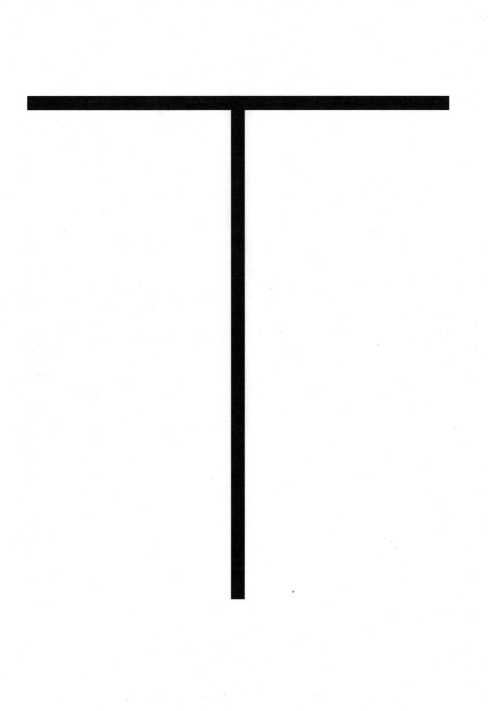

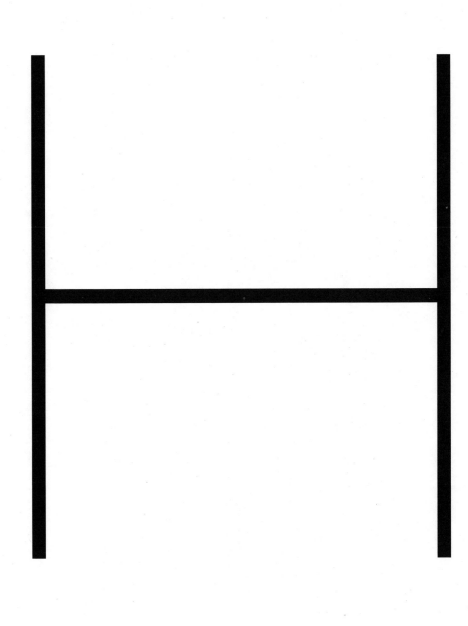

ANDREW JORON

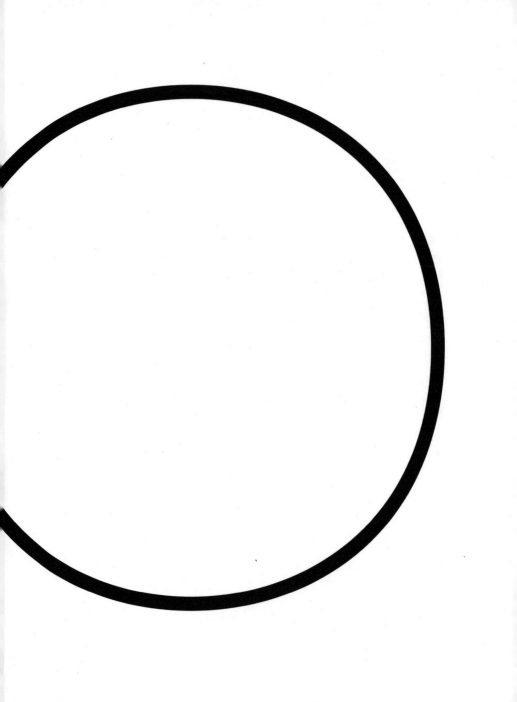

Designed by Quemadura
Black Square Editions
1200 Broadway, Suite 3C
New York, New York 10001

These poems have been previously published in the following periodicals: *Abacus, Angle,*
Aufgabe, The Avec Sampler, Etherdome Broadside Series, Facture, The Germ, Hambone,
Mirage #4/Periodical, New American Writing, Skanky Possum, Sulfur, Untitled and *Urvox.*

1

POUR RROSE

THE EMERGENCY

1

What good is poetry at a time like this? It feels right to ask this question, and at the same time to resist the range of predictable answers, such as: Poetry is useless, therein lies its freedom. Or, poetry has the power to expose ideology; gives a voice to that which has been denied a voice; serves as a call to action; consoles and counsels; keeps the spirit alive.

All of the above answers are true, yet somehow inadequate. This is because poetry cannot be anything other than inadequate, even to itself. Where language fails, poetry begins. Poetry forces language to fail, to fall out of itself, to become something other than itself—

A kind of topological fold or failure (called a "catastrophe" in mathematics) precedes the emergence—constitutes the emergency—of the New. If poetry "makes language new," then it must be defined as the translation of emergency. Even politically engaged poetry cannot escape this consequence. The abyssal language of poetry represents (translates) the motion of social change more than it does the facts of social change.

Language is a social construct, yet it was fashioned by no one in particular. Language continues to be haunted by this "no one." Indeed, the basic structures of language have more in common with molecular bonds than with human interactions.

To the extent that words are things, they cannot speak. (Speaking belongs to social action.) Poetry, before taking action, listens to the speechlessness of words.

Receiver of the sender who is "no one." (As the initial shading out of nothing, the sending of the longest amplitude—the deepest, the slowest —is always a lament.)

2

At this moment (late 2001), public space in the United States is bedecked with flags, colorfully curtaining the contradictions of the "war against terrorism," which is itself a higher, officially sanctioned form of terrorism.

"America stands united," yet remains a divided and antagonistic society, driven by capitalism's war of all against all. Such a society can achieve "unity" only through hatred of an external enemy. This is the utopian aspect of military campaigns.

But the euphoria of this new-found unity is fading fast. The screens have been repaired, but the picture still doesn't look right. Civil liberties have been curtailed, while new rights and benefits have been granted to the big corporations. Moreover, the "war of good against evil" seems to entail U.S. support for undemocratic regimes and clandestine organizations, hardly differing from those of the purported enemy, to the extent that such forces enable U.S. capital and influence to penetrate a given region of the world.

In the Mideast, in particular, acts of resistance to U.S. domination have grown increasingly desperate. Needless to say, no grievance could justify the atrocities committed on 9/11. These horrific acts constituted nothing less than crimes against humanity—to which the U.S. was obligated, morally and politically, not to respond in kind. A civilized nation would have investigated and prosecuted the crimes according to procedures laid down by international law. Instead, the U.S. chose to violate the law by conducting a war of annihilative vengeance, caring very little to discriminate between suspected terrorists and innocent bystanders.

—only an inert and mechanical prose can accommodate these events. It would be barbaric to write a poem about them, to use them for aesthetic purposes—

The United States, in its all-consuming pursuit of wealth and power, "has rained death and destruction on more people in more regions of the globe than any other nation in the period since the Second World War" (*Monthly Review*, November 2001). Violence of this order must take its toll on the life-world of the destroyer-nation itself. A harsh, acrid odor begins to seep through the walls, spoiling works of art and other fixtures of civilization.

In the case of America, this odor appears to be invigorating.—Adorno believed that any civilization guilty of mass murder must forfeit its right to cultural creation. As he famously declared, "To write poetry after Auschwitz is barbaric." In his view, aesthetic practices that once prefigured social emancipation now serve only to mask or to legitimate systemic violence. Here in America, however, "culture" has been reduced to a simple play of intensities, to the simultaneously brutal and sentimental pulsions of mass media. Any "legitimation function" would be superfluous: the American machine, with its proudly exposed components of Accumulation and Repression, has no need for such a carapace.

American poetry is a marginal genre whose existence is irrelevant to the course of Empire. Yet here, only here, at this very juncture between language and power, can the refused word come back to itself as the word of refusal, as the sign of that which cannot be assimilated to the system—

Word that opens a solar eye in the middle of the Night.

Opens, but fails to dispel the dark. Of necessity, perhaps, because it fails necessity itself. Opens, if only to make an O, an indwelling of zero, an Otherness.

The creative Word comes into its exile here, in the world's most destructive nation.

This poetic opening in the "real world" is a wonderful (meaning miraculous) wound, a sigh more than a sign. It has none of the decorative quality of the art of forgetting; this Word does not bring reconciliation. It affirms nothing but the negative truth of its non-identity. It does not communicate at all, except to announce the incommunicable, as abyssal groan, as *Ungrund.*

This shudder makes itself felt in the oldest, shamanic art, in labor turned against itself, toward the production of—the distribution of—[say here what spills spells: that Word that goes wanting]. Yet it also represents an expenditure that must be regulated. Polarized by the field of social struggle, *poiesis* is pulled at once toward the ornamental and the abyssal.

Ornament raises possibilities in order to restrict them. It has no hold, however, on the release of the Cry. The limited cannot attain the limitless, except by a *sudden break.*

Adorno himself conceded, some years after his initial statement, that "Perennial suffering has as much right to expression as a tortured man has to scream; hence it may have been wrong to say that after Auschwitz you could no longer write poems."

Yet the Cry involves more than a reflexive response to pain: it is an act of creation, a sign that the world is not equal to itself.

Haven't the very bones of language, in which meaning is always displaced from its object, the structure of a lament? Isn't this lament already evident in every self-separation, every self-exceeding motion of matter? What did Adorno know about the blues, and their ancient authority?

The blues, all blues, are the matrix of the world's subaltern cultures, an expression of triumph in defeat. The raising of the voiceless voice, *omnipresent roar of that river forced underground.*

(The more ancient the blues, the more collective the voice.)

Today's evidence: bare branches at the winter solstice, the turning point. The word to be awaited here.

Word beyond meaning—for that which triumphs in defeat is the Inexpressible, the joyous object of lament. All of language, as a mode of interaction that never is fully present to itself, amounts to the labor of producing this object.

The *emergence* of this object constitutes an *emergency* for any restricted economy of meaning. The privileged site of such an emergency in language is the poem, where something ontologically unprecedented springs forth: *Der Rätsel ist Reinentsprungenes* (the enigma is pure springing-forth), as Hölderlin testified.

This "enigma"—the poem's saying of the unsayable—arises from the interaction of a particular set of words, yet its enigmatic properties cannot be located among the properties of its constituent elements (i.e., the meanings of the words). The enigma springs forth purely at the level of interaction, and so exceeds the reality of the interacting elements themselves.

Indeed, scientists as well as poets now speculate that the origin of language itself was an "innovation" that "would have depended on the phenomenon of emergence, whereby a chance combination of preexisting elements results in something totally unexpected. The classic example of an emergent quality is water, most of whose remarkable characteristics are entirely unpredicted by those of its constituents, hydrogen and oxygen. Nonetheless, the combination of these ingredients gives rise to something entirely new, and expected only in hindsight." Thus, "we have to conclude that the appearance of language was not driven by natural selection" (*Scientific American*, December 2001)—instead, like water, language also is an emergent phenomenon, spontaneously springing forth as a pure enigma, an overflowing of reality, a surreality.

Recent studies of complex systems (from which the concept of emergence is derived) appear to confirm the surrealist insight into the poetic-revolutionary nature of reality. Investigations have shown that systems comprised of a large number of elements far from equilibrium are prone to beautiful convulsions called "phase transitions." In this process, chance associations within the system, after reaching a critical point, undergo spontaneous self-organization. At this point, the Novum—*an unexpected, unprecedented superaddition to reality*—emerges. Here is the dynamical equivalent of water flowing uphill: the system increases its complexity (and temporarily contravenes entropy) by incorporating chaos. The origins of order are vertiginous: by "riding" its own chaotic tendencies, the system propels itself to a higher level of organization. Complex systems, as one researcher put it, are situated at the "edge of chaos."

Within the complex system of language, a word's meaning is "edged"— and chaotically conditioned—by the meanings of all other words. Communication attempts to crystallize this chaos by establishing fixed relations between the meanings of particular words. But such language-crystals melt and reform constantly in response to their (subjectively mediated) surroundings. (Complex systems are typically open systems to which rigid concepts of "inside" and "outside" do not apply. Such openness allows them to be extremely sensitive to changes in the environment.) In this process, communication proves susceptible to structural failure. The abyssal turbulence of language as a whole, always brimming beneath the surface of stabilized meaning, can initiate a spontaneous phase transition that accelerates words far beyond equilibrium, toward the condition of poetry.

Poetry is the self-organized criticality of the cry.

(The concept of "self-organized criticality" can be illustrated by pouring a quantity of sand onto a tabletop: the fallen particles will build up into a conical pile. This shape is the product of self-organization, for the pile maintains itself around a critical vertex, a balance-point between order and chaos. Once this critical point is reached, the effect of a single particle's impact on the pile no longer can be predicted. One particle may cause a chain reaction of cascades upon impact, while another may rest where it falls. Not only have the system's elements spontaneously organized themselves in reaction to an influx of energy, but the system as a whole has "tuned" itself toward a state of criticality, where single events have the widest possible range of effects.)

A poem tunes itself toward a state of criticality, a condition of language in which single words have the widest possible range of effects. No matter how the poem has been constructed, when *poiesis* has been achieved, the words of the poem leap spontaneously to a new interactive level (irreducible to any previous level), a level representing the self-organization of a cry emanating from nowhere and no one, but pervading all of language. What disequilibrium forces this *original cry* to wander through countless subsystems of meaning, always exceeding the capacities of each to contain it, until it finally surpasses the system of language itself?

4

When laments are raised, they run together like water, collecting into a river that rushes toward an unknown ocean. They travel always in the direction of lengthening shadows, merging in the collectivity of night.

According to human-rights groups, the number of civilians (mostly women, children, and old people) killed by U.S. bombing in Afghanistan now equals the number of people killed by the terrorist attacks on 9/11. Once again, vengeful acts have taken the lives of three thousand innocent people. The U.S. has responded to a crime against humanity by inflicting another, equally atrocious one. Furthermore, the relentless bombing has halted the delivery of humanitarian aid, placing millions of refugees in imminent danger of disease and starvation.

Through the night of these sacred and profane wars of vengeance, the words of a poet must come together with those of others struggling for peace and social justice. Words of anger, argument, and analysis especially are needed, for these words lead to action. But the oldest, deepest oppositional words are those issued in lament. The lament, no less than anger, refuses to accept the fact of suffering. But while anger must possess the stimulus of a proximate cause—or else it eventually fades away—the lament has a universal cause, and rises undiminished through millennia of cultural mediation. Unlike anger, the lament survives translation into silence, into ruins.

Contemporary lyricism has been described as the "singing of song's impossibility." This, too, may be a version of the blues—whose strong ontological claim (to manifest the spontaneous emergence—or emergency—of an unprecedented Cry) now must be renewed.

Such a renewal would constitute an "ontological turn" away from the epistemological dilemmas of modern and postmodern poetics, where poetry is understood to emerge from the questioning of poetry. To the extent that a question anticipates its answer, it is unprepared to receive the Novum. That which is radically *other* does not reveal itself under interrogation.

The *deep blues*, then, are not a mode of questioning, but arrive in advance of doubt—and represent a negation more primary than doubt.

Here is the seed of all resistance. Here is its ratio:

$$\frac{\text{O, the grieving vowel}}{\text{zero, the mouth of astonishment}}$$

5

In a word, the uncanny reflection of an unfinished world.

FATHOM

1

Climb to climate, the awe of O's
Fiery circumference.

Not to justify this (spillage of integers).
Not to be eaten but spoken (as a "seed" or a "seeming").

Muscular skill, the red-rippling
Curtains, the deep interior of the play.

The motions all unrehearsed
Lunar risings, slow crescendos, cries against God—

  a self-refuting silence.

Commentary

The finest jest is made "in advance of" the jester.

A new generation of snails, with "eyes that are horns of the moon"—

"The Propositions," *The Distances.*

Here a plagiarist assumes the place of the author.

2

Earth rose
In a gown of white air

On the morning of an endless night.
Soundless as the Book

—a bone Garden of artificial sound.
The desert's listening instrument—

At this game of decay's cadences
You win your second skin.

An empty repetition initiates the series.

Commentary

—ciphers, sapphires. *Veers* round & round *reveres.*

Reading is an act of intervention that remains blank—whose immobility (re)joins writing at the very moment of its (always unrealized) origin.

Writing's blood is invisible but meant to be red.

A memory of the Not-Yet (abandoned city). At its center, there stands a misshapen statue of living minerals, neither natural nor artificial. Everywhere the light aims at a vanishing point: now is the late hour of the commentary.

3

What fateful door hinges
On the difference between "shall" & "will"?

All *shall* vanish into their futurity.
None *will* question their intent.

The face of the Other who refuses to wake
Resembles a clock.

That entry was lost, that was the entrance
To this Time of writing—

where the eyes of effacement were hoarded.

Commentary

If, in reading, we "invite the shadow," we press a word to reveal its lost priority—

Such tension has its characteristic color: a star striated throughout the folds of flesh.

Here, the subject is allowed to walk backward into the mirror of subjection.

Here, the decanted words flow back into the vessel's mouth.

4

All forgetting—is fear?—is Sphere?—
No, gashed negation—

Furious weather that wants to fill the world.
Is signal's running down to *single*'s many—

A head to inhabit—
A heart repealing laws like a ceaseless bell.

"Fathom" as heading, or imperative
Ceremonial to the human embryo: a brilliant fish.

—*usk'm mot, inthessi, inthessi, usk'm mot.*

Commentary

All translation is treasonous (as in "Never will I renounce the necessity of Communism, nor of my desire for architecture to dissolve into structures of music. . . .")

Here is a caesura of years lengthening into (relative) strangeness, composed in a soft medium that keeps a record of every injury.

"Speech," then, is no more than a plight of displaced ground left here by the Great Transparent Ones: a half-completed ruin moving sideways in time.

An involuted, an involuntary mechanism, answering this and this and this.

5 *for Barbara Guest*

To shatter "craniology," liberate "crane"
Where a presence affords—an unfelt shudder.

An urging along door-, then deer-haunted corridors
Pranked with salt, & psalteries.

That "roof"
Invited this "proof"—now an interstellar object

Now a parlor of belated events. Bodies to be
Studied, perhaps steadied by ardor.

Encastled in what mirage, awaiting—

Commentary

—what marriage of Translation & betrayal.

"Nothing can be revoked." This phrase now has no referent but a utopian island.

O—the last degradation of Eros, also known as "the grieving vowel." Ritual that rises out of order, many-chambered number zero.

One by one, the senses are multiplied: speech-spiral, wound on wound, a platform for suspended fire.

6

FATUM stands cold & fantastical—
As a sentence never invented.

Saith the scythe—
X equals this (excision).

Bird-encircled column, assassin's robes.
Quietness—a null choir—

A non-repeating pattern of tiles.
A non-political motive.

—*victorious banner raised above the toppled state.*

Commentary

Essentialist (to the point of denying motion).

Orientalist.

Illuminated (eliminated) by rash conclusions (by clouds).

How the vernacular vibrates here: artful only in its refusal to submit to the work of breathing.

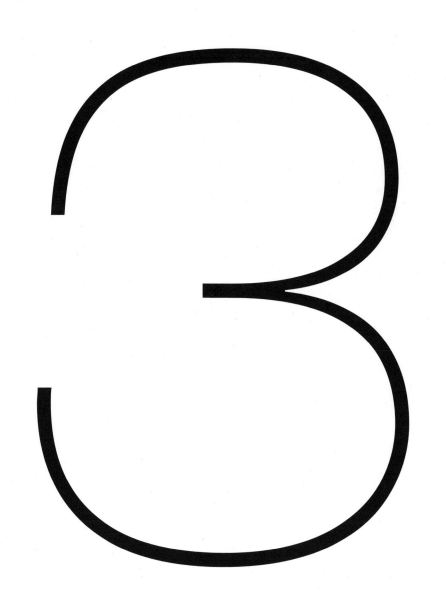

CONSTELLATIONS

FOR THEREMIN

Poppy and Remembrance

CELAN

                      Dream-herb

                      GOLL

This cycle of twelve prose poems offers a commentary on, and a translation of, certain passages from the poems of Paul Celan and Yvan Goll—namely, those passages submitted as evidence of Celan's alleged plagiarism of Goll.

The charges against Celan are examined most thoroughly—and refuted unconditionally—in an article by Reinhard Döhl in the 1960 Jahrbuch of the Deutsche Akademie für Sprache und Dichtung. The epigraphs below, presenting twelve "parallel instances" wherein Celan's lines seem to echo Goll's, have been drawn from this article.

Rather than confirming plagiarism, the "parallel instances" testify to a marvellous confluence between Celan's early and Goll's late work. In the wake of the controversy, however, this moment of solidarity—of mutual inspiration—between the two poets has been minimized. Yet it is worth remembering that Celan personally delivered a copy of his first book to Goll and so initiated an earnest exchange of texts and talks. Celan recalls in a letter (to Alfred Margul-Sperber) that he visited Goll "many times," even as Goll's leukemia worsened. On these occasions, Celan would read his new work aloud to the dying poet. According to Celan, "The fact that Goll, who for many years hadn't written in German, began, before his death, to write in German again, is due in no small measure to his connection with me and my poems."

Consequently, the echoic qualities of the passages in question must be understood in a redemptive light, as examples of Breton's alchemical vases communicants. To recover and reintegrate the utopian substance of these wounded words, an elaborate apparatus has been assembled here.

Its main component is the theremin, the electronic lyre of the Russian Revolution. This instrument is equipped with two antennas that generate an electromagnetic field; the performer's hands, without touching any surface, move within the field in an artful manner, causing a ripple of interference that, in turn, stimulates an oscillator to produce musical tones. The vital power radiated by the antique kithara—to animate stones (Amphion's lyre) or to rescue the dead (Orpheus's lyre)—is ascribed here to the theremin.

The epigraphs are intended, therefore, to function as the antennas of an imaginary theremin. Their "etheric waves" cascade over the body of the text below, activating its constituent elements. (The text is made up of both commentaries and translations. The latter derive from the same poems as the epigraphs and are marked by quotes. Translations from Goll's source-poems are given in the third paragraph of each section; from Celan's, in the fourth. But these boundaries are not impermeable, and phrases from the source-poems are liable to circulate throughout each section.)

Caught in an etheric field, the translations and commentaries interact as "constellations," in Benjamin's sense of a non-hierarchical, indeed, a salvational structure of thought. At once philosophical and poetical, the constellation unites—without abolishing the differences between—its nodal elements. It is a necessarily musical relation that prefigures the moment of reconciliation.

with birds in his hair he goes forth

CELAN

Your flesh of rose—your hair of birds

GOLL

That birds become points or musical notes; & that hair, horizontal lines or staves...

Hands are entangled in a force field to make music.
Hands are birds caught in the hair of the theremin.

"The closer I approach you, the more you sink into the abyss of pre-existant objects."

"In vain you paint hearts on the window: a god goes among the hordes."

Flights of birds tune the strings of a destroyed or not-yet- invented instrument.

Pictures of ancient noise, hieratic news. Suggesting hair, birds, & the blue banners of the invisible.

the mills of death

<small>CELAN</small>

The Mill of Death

<small>GOLL</small>

A wheel-inhabited house. That adversary knows only advance: that cycle moves as this sickle.

Alter, altar. All beyond feeling, number than Blakean number, blacker than fact or factory.

"The fire turns pale, along with the water. There, on death's negative, blanches the cedar with carbonized branches."

"... doing the work better left to one's star."

That which spreads "beneath mammalian sleep"; that which swears "loudly from the rooftops of dreamless sleep."

As a theremin quotes from the Book of Disquiet: to see the sun at night, the eye pours out its contents.

A necklace of hands

CELAN

A necklace of larksongs

GOLL

The first book holds the letters of the last. Never to be corrected or corrupted, but thrown into the mouth of earth.

Memory is reduced to monument; unseen weight that bends the poppy, a perennial herb with milky juice, also known as the dreaming herb.

"We walk toward the single great eye that hangs over clouds in the forehead of a sullen thinker."

"Shells do I utter and thin clouds, and a hull sprouts in the rain . . . Black the portal springs open, I sing."

Fate foretold in tallow light: "silent circling lamps" lend a deeper hue to the jar of wasps, the bottle of air.

Voice, never-arriving wave. The sound of the theremin sorrows over the absolute whiteness of the sick man's blood.

blood-ray of the moon

CELAN

a drop of moon-blood

GOLL

Cast into temporal waters, the bright broken images seek to rejoin, to become Original.

What lies open to reflection? The unanswered word, the world before it was made.

"Your foot will forget its way of going ... planted my herb potent with magic ... You must love me whether you want to or not."

"We say obscure things to one another, we love one another like poppy and remembrance."

"It's time that it was time" to drink one red drop, to sleep as wine in the shells.

See the sea misalign its mimic heaven! Song for theremin: "We are friends." Voice, never-returning wave.

Magic cannot be seen or named. Better to banish the word, or show how black sublates white: as the German *rein*, the French *rien*.

Consider the line, with its mutually exclusive endpoints. To be exiled is the true homecoming. What, then, is the nature of self- evidence?

"And you and I with starry crowns: Proof eternal against the doom of time."

"So that a ripening like yours will enrapture the festive Eye that has wept such stones."

In this tale of the body, errors accumulate without fail. Victory tomorrow will be measured by the sun's refusal to rise.

Slavery will end, as the peripatetic argued, when the Loom weaves without a hand to guide it, or when the Lyre plays itself.

the mauve-colored death

CELAN

la mort violette

GOLL

To observe the paradox of a death *qui porte un nom de fleur,* divide appearance from its petal.

Then gaslights will burn as "reverberant flowers whose bereavement is mauve" or "wakeful flowers of the first sleep of the dead."

You, the other, always died. As someone said, "with a French heart, a German mind, and Jewish blood." But "you did not die the mauve-colored death."

You awaited the half-night's "dream-daggers," giving a "cry not from pain." After fighting your way deeper down, liberated, you were found by a fisherman on the holiday of revolution.

If there is a word that marks the place where language was born, it is "you."

Violated / violet. Now everything has been said: the theremin modulates as ethereal violin, fantastic prayer.

seven hearts later the hand knocks at the gate,
seven roses later the fountain splashes.

CELAN

You have seven hearts, queen,
They are all ignited
And compose my crown

GOLL

As talk, forced bleeding through higher dimensions, evolves toward ty-
pography, limbs pinned awkwardly to thin air.

Out of sequence, a Nilotic cat comes home to electricity, slinking past
shifting deserts of meaning.

"The first rose is of granite. The second rose is of red wine. The third rose is
of lark feathers. The fourth rose is of rust. The fifth rose is of longing. The
sixth rose is of tin. But the seventh—the most delicate, the devout, the noc-
turnal, the sisterly—shall grow, immediately following your death, out of
your tomb."

"Seven nights higher red migrates to red." Here is no halt for identities,
only a blue recognition of distances beyond blue.

How time stands still for a thrower of shadows! How empty of doubt, the
fullness of Adamic speech . . .

The purest coincidence of system & accident.

I place the ashen flower, its darkness
fully grown, under glass.

CELAN

Within my ashen masks
The lights are extinguished.

GOLL

The apprehension of voices in a darkened room. One word between them. The thing not signaled or hidden; neither feared nor received.

Deceleration is the way to beauty. As measures lengthen, the insufficiencies show their lacework, their oceanic openings.

Thus, "an owl in vestments of night" is called to brood the ovum of a dying soul; and "a late bird" carries, all summer long, "the ice-grain in its beak."

What writing erases: a man, standing "on the threshold of the withered hour," decides to enter, compelled by "the drums of the final hour."

Recto, a plaster bust of the poet reciting, *verso*, with an unreal "sister-mouth," an admonition to virtue.

The burn of whiteness / witness. The book a scene of heavy curtains, wind-inhabited.

The moon was hacked to bits

The moon-axe
Sinks into my marrow.

Unhealed untreated. The spilled goblet, under the spell of lunar gravity, floats to the floor. An accident of the blood; the waters superimposed on purpose.

Man-made mother, eroded word: body peering through the body.

"Terminal olive tree, my skeleton rises out of the Asiatic wastes." The first book opens as song in the wasteland; the last one laments & accuses its maker. "The foreign heart is hung, phosphorescent, in my ribcage."

To come to the city of the abandoned body, the book to come. Or to "drink from wooden bowls the ashes of the fountains" of an unknown city. "How is it that I still live? Uncertain god, to prove you to yourself."

Violation of, as method: extinct voice in the cistern.

Being divided by itself alone. The theremin interprets: the sonic flowerfall of primes.

The suns of death are white

CELAN

a sacred dagger slashes our death-sun

GOLL

The crisis of the object creates an image without analogy. From reference to face to face: *between* will bind its twin, or twist detail to overarching feature.

Such words must turn inside out in order to stay the same.

"The cry, the human cry out of the lightless body that like a sacred dagger slashes our death-sun." Solar cry that according to Copernicus inhabits the center of every voice.

"The suns of death are white like the hair of our child, who climbs out of the flood as you pitch a tent upon the dunes. Our child, who brandishes the knife of happiness over us with extinguished eyes."

Mergence of crime & cry in "the crisis of the object." An emergency everlasting. Hands shy away from this immaculate damage; the same hands hover over the throat of the theremin.

Scratched-out script: bloodline of unstable constellations.

Black milk of early morning

CELAN

The red milk of strength

GOLL

The complete works: the crumpled plan.

The long breath brought to term.

"Woman, anti-woman, rise out of your occult prehistory to exert your double dominion ... Androgyne, solar moon ... For the love of nothing, in a card game pitting one against the other, marry and betray the Ego-world."

"A grave in the winds ... a grave in the clouds ... play death more sweetly ... scrape the fiddles more darkly ... then you will rise as smoke ... death is a master from Germany."

Each bell-howl, as skin-stretched-sky & industry.

Land peopled by pillars. Chorus, the irrevocable.

The white heart of our world

CELAN

to find the heart of the world

GOLL

Mazed interior. This curving wall has one side only.

Here, a calm contemplative terror is applied to patterns—to polyps whose tentacles are polyps with tentacles.

"Where water stirs, there night dives in, expecting to find the heart of the world."

"The sea's ink-blackness around the mouth ... Brow that broods over shells and waves ... beautiful, in place of the heart ... O knocking, that comes and goes! In finitude undulate the veils."

What smoulders in the smallest cell: the groan of *against,* the shudder of great negation.

Answering quiet to send / uncanny echo to question.

Trance Archive

"No" goes
Where the war of analogy allows—
"Stop" to start, "house" to walk roofless & aflame.

In *Principia*, the solid of least resistance
is language—Moon
More earthlike than the Earth.

Prose is the ocean of that shore—
that, unauthored, revises & erases
its propositions.

New entry under "singing" or "singeing"—
lines closed or disclosed
under accelerating clouds.

Only the fingertips of the eyes
Can touch this distance.
It is a kind of cold fire.

What surplus is hidden
In the place of in the place of?
Mirror, to remain unmoved, divides its answer.

So light itself, thrown into fact, opposes
everything revealed.
Unravelled thread: the letter's perfect Form.

As talk opaques the breath—
Tenebrae aches in the mark of the marrow.
The plural to violate the verb, verbless to bless.

Troubled, bled traceries in series
as the downed sound dawned.
All's aligned, annulled, annealed, axioms

made anxious in imitation of vanishing.
Accidental universal—
The imperative to pour, poor, pure, to no purpose.

Again an agony of
like paired with like, skin
pared from fruit, no

Vaster than its voiceprint, standing still
To escape itself
    instead of dancing like a skeleton.

Echo
    that precedes the call, the premise.
White moth, whiter mother forever called away—

"No" goes to no beginning. The audience of the dead
    gathers at this barrier, this
    deafening defining, writing—

No, volume
    whose head is cleaved, that leaks an inkling
    of last things.

"No" goes to "noise" then to "ghost."
To separate corrupted curtains, to open the book
    behind the book—

Spine to Spin,
Spoke to Speak

The pilot alone knows
That the plot is missing its
Eye.

Why isn't this "ominous science"
    itself afraid, a frayed
Identity?

Pray, protagonist—
Prey to this series of staggered instants.

Here the optic
Paints its hole, its self-consuming moment.
It is speech, dispelled, that
    begs to begin to ache.

So that *wind* accelerates to *wound*, a dead sound
    enlivened by the visitation of owls.

As pallid as parallel, the cry
Of the negative is not the negative
    of the cry—an irreparable blessing—

A green world's
    "sibilant shadows" where
The syllables of your name are growing younger.

As involuntary as involuted, "who"
    returns its noun
    to each tender branch
That *noon* breaks into *no one.*

Point of view
Hovers, a circular cloud, over evacuated
Time.

That heard its herd bellow below
    the terraced cities, the milled millions

as sold as unsouled, ghost-cargos.

A symptom of the Maddening—
Woman undressed of her flesh.
Man's address
    to Thou, & the flag of Thou.

How the fallen state

Meets the starry horizon, veil

    against witness, hunger against void.

O, oldest

    outermost Other—

Ageing mask

Of the transparent Earth. Unspeculated

    image

Streaked with mirror & stricken words.

You are neither the torn, nor the thorn.

You are the many-petalled

    melting point of repeating decimals . . .

Receiver, river

Has been burned into voice, a day-dark ribbon.

All signal is this

Single.

Mazed Interior

1

Cogs & cogs that cannot turn
    to recognitions: such dogs in the dark noonday!

As if the tongue told & tolled
Among
    the melancholic arcades.

Where the *moods* advance toward the *modes*.

Time to try the knot, the Not
Or to be caught
Forever in nerve-traceries of Beauty . . .

Unstrung, the structure is sound.

2

Detour to far fires.

To be counted missing . . . in a toroidal space
That mimics the shape of its container, speech.

The passive of, the possessive of—

Measureless intent, *blue* almost *black*, the picture
     below the voice.
Less a name than a substance

Coming to stillness, star-inhabited.
Less a substance than a sigh.

3

Awaited, thou, *unawaited*. Divided here. O

     then
Opened as earthen
     ring, cave-recorded.

A mazed interior. Self-similar aisles of isles, pouring
form from form.

Lastness as device. Aligned as measurements (letters)—

as sensitive, all-too-sensitive compass
needles forever seeking
the frozen pole, the zero.

Caption: "An end-of-century sailing ship, *Delirium*
held fast in sheets of ice."

4

No atmosphere is sufficient.

An embryo in the brain is not yet breathing.

There, the labor
Of the living rock, where an ache, or bruise-ember
will be discovered.

Scored
for Theremin, or permanently scarred.

Where shadows point: *Mad* lengthening to *made*, as unmade
   scaffolding.

   Thus, repetition, resisted
   is the register of thought.
Now here, even as staves are falling, another story

—intervallic—cannot be told—that is, besieged

As the heart encaged in bone.

The animal calls *long long*, disconsolate
In its hollow mountain.

   5

Neither nor nor neither, time builds
Its twelve tones between *round* & *ruined.*

—as the roots of the sunflower, arrayed over earthlight.

Routes unreturning / term without terminus. Riding as reading
Migrates
   underground.

Writing as the righting
Of fallen
    angles, of tangles of Accident—

    arrives riven, a body never to be / surveyed.

Abandoned in a wintry field, the sum of its travels

—its hunting the same as its haunting.

Dolphy at Delphi

for Garrett Caples

No lesson but a lessening, a loosening.
The spiral is made to spill its center.

—a name that acts—imperative's axe
Loses its head

As a baritone (the low
    solo's slow slope) sax (imaginary
    gender needs no sleep).

How the wrong notes compose their own song

Parallel to a dream of drowned cities.

After hours, what style of address, what robes
    (robs us
Of daylight) of delight?

Tells, then shows
The *revel* hidden in *reveal*?

—now's even later than the future. Found
sound reduced to meaning.

The perpetual emotion of a star-like story.

The Book Is
an Abstract Candle

Avian V
Above, below
    disturbance of the thinking reed.

Look that stirs stars—
Answering reflection.

The *whiteness* not yet bled dry.

"The problem of content"
    is this prayer.
First & last, uncanny sentinels
Visible only to the voice.

To distinguish sound from its shadow—

To extinguish, then
    to quell

The cold equations—candle
   & marrow, blood & burning.

An apprehension, as of symbols—
An intense repose

   pages the moments: ages the mirages.

(To be turned toward facelessness.)

Where, exfoliated of exile—
Words are uncreated mouths, music corrupted
   into meaning.

Perhaps the geometry of a lament—
The travail
   of Earth's *intellectual surface*
   chambered with doubt.

A weighted wood, a conditional

That leaves leaves
   to the seasons later than winter

   —seasons of seizures & caesuras.

Konvolut N

The Law of the Father is an umbral voice.

The umbral voice is a feather
    falling to earth.

      abraded earth, cumulus of

      [*a cancelled line*]

—braided around
The law of falling water—

Its utterance
    received by
An inverted landscape, or sunken sky.

The record of the voice
    is another line—
A desert "crowded into a corridor."

—a cord that does not correspond
But suspends.

The chord, also, is a vanishing relation.

The last line
    listens to its endlessness.

What Spills Spells

1. The Spoils

Neither raven nor haven, but a sound-drowned line.

All hollowed, no name is news to a drum.

The complete sentence holds its antlers high, antennae tuned to distant static.

Here a cloud is seeking a crowd, a clown a crown.

As "we," apparently ageless, converge upon a place of no resistance. Many words remain missing.

Now one of them—"rose"—appears to raise the dead. To the stillness inside the story.

Whose mouth—exponent of zero—repeats this order, aping the natural mask whose picture nominates speech.

To *hold* what is *holed*: reason's trapezoidal portrait.

The twin of (the body of) *between*.

In other words: appearance is a blind spot, a space of turbulence caused by an actor walking into a mirror—

Is, then, a "shine of recession" always to be posed against the interrogative? Perhaps.

2. The Spools

"Vanishing into visibility" is considered circus-like today.

Believer, return to the first erasure.

Resurrected for a hooded audience, a bird-winged book.

How a phrase freezes when sun-struck. To be illustrated by mourning, morning, and the abstractions induced by winter.

Doubt fills the margin of the page (confession of nudity).

Face averted, lacking every commentary. Soiled evidence, in ceaseless arrival—

Either "there is no time" or "there is no time."

How the mystical tenet *turns faster than* the groan of regret. This, within the same wheel of words.

Writing as the art of reading as rewriting.

"Drink me," says the dramatic sky. But there is no school for red weather, and the Moon shines with a borrowed light.

The hidden handprint is always represented.

3. The Spalls

So goes the *via negativa*. After the likeness of—

A riverbed (a porous science).

Alluvial fan opening meaning. Defined by, defied by, deified by, one word deposited upon another. Neither source nor mouth, but a crossed-out sacrifice.

How "the myth" is deposited upon "the mouth"—

Uncollected images of—

A rock's reckless reckoning. After magic, contingency itself appoints the letter A.

To Be Explained

A basic code's deliberate error.
Five gyrating holes, inborn.

A motherless sun at night—
Overheard behind the wall of sound.

The rude red road that
Leads backward into the body.

A fiery animal that lives inside the eye.
Magnetism ebbing from the hands.

The coming war's ghosts
Already preserved in black & white.

The orrery of ideas.
The ossuary of things.

The phoneme shared by ash & erasure.
The compass that points toward an unfinished world.

Astronomy, music, dialectics.
Arrayed negations, the intervals between appearances.

Always toylike in the telling—
The angles kneeling in mute witness.

A myriad displacements
Not to be explained.

Poem for
Sotère Torregian

What, then
Avails this—signless sleep, or extending
The veil to this vale?

Repetition
Shines for no reason, then
For no reason.
To refute the river's burden of sameness.

The will is a wall
That stands for finitude.

To banish—only an act of will.
To vanish—only a verb without an object.

Given what is
To be given
Never again.

A speaking whirlwind—a wail or a well
Deeper than space.
Whose premise here is the defiance of proof.

Communication with Drowned Souls

So deep
That motions become blessings.

Below the danger of—

How unlike a weapon
That leaps into the hand, a thought.

A system of thought
Shifting in relation to—

Now, *cloak*
Approaches *clock* like a prayer.

Hued, as in air; hewed, as in stone.

Where bells of
dissonance are still
Half-submerged in *distance.*

Where the quickening of *eyes* equals *ice.*

Always departing
In never-to-be-repeated patterns.

Furious, the frozen moment
whose fractures
teach accident & order.

Why is there something rather than nothing?

The bottomlessness
of things is answered only
by a question.

The Evening of Chances

The leveling of chants is—

The etching of, the evening of, irregular glows. The various chases. The chastening glove.

Pay attention: *the of is*, space, experience, emptiness.

No, slower than silence. Reward to reword, word-whirled world.

Frameless, the real is what we cannot look away from.

Every cause is an accident: so blue, trembling, awaits its turn.

Against begins, nudity without body.

Blue sister, who shows us how to disturb her rest. Revealed in the grain: this deviance grown absolute.

Sheets of motion—writing—the blade that bleeds.

As the senses multiply, we look away to contemplate.

As the rains relate to ruins, as the bells—As the bells, bells, bells, bells, bells, bells, bells—

Can sameness answer its own secret? Here, the rains relate to ruins, & a dead tree has walked across the desert.

Such pauses repeat, but never return. Structure stretches into content, as trace over trance.

Let X represent the human cipher in a pose of astonishment. The future past is understood: we will have existed.

Understood here means *unsheltered*: not stood under. Similar to a prayer's elongated figure.

Cold noise collects in the listening devices. All blues & sciences.

Eclipse Calling

0.

Poured orbit, O
An all-rounding river of last regard

Given nothing for
Given

Cannot rest, but runs in countercurrents
    against

    that pax, that poverty of state—

As contorted as letters
The bodies lie still below the readable surface.

1.

To those who—come to comb rayed musics
Out of matter—read

Red eddies, desire as Swan, as swoon of dawn—
Commune
of all that cannot be thought:

Earth & blood are even, because Divisible.
Heaven
Is odd, because indivisible. So free from prayer.

—a free word says death or, better, death
To the president.

Imagine the spoken, O's
Spokes convergent on no center. No place
Is polis
but there are violins preceding violence.
A word is birthplace of the plural body.

As wide-eyed as wild-isled:
  I & I
  achieving signature upon inverted landscape-sky.

Accepted into vastly revolving ocean
As shock of nudity—

  that posture foaming to far pasture, to pure field.

Here, first person is maintained: an archaic device, somehow
  stopped inside its own velocity, its substance
  dissimilar to itself—

Its living moment: relic of a movement unarriving.

2.

Of *if* born of *of,* there is no information—
  the universal is unsaved.

Age to come to calm
  if & only if
Calm's measure makes disquiet.

For a phrase = a fragile thread
Composed of something dead, plus pulse.

O my Other, mother-throated One—
Name, between
    abandoned body—
        the twin of *of*.

Horn fight, drum fight, drafting tatters in the head.

The groan as ground-tone is also known.
    Unsaved is this
    unstruck instrument. A theater, someday with tall voices

        —chorus overboiling like cumuli—will be lifted from the sea.

From *frees* to *free*, the verbs do not agree.

Shadow
    belongs to the half that is always hungry.

Totality's ring
    a window-effect
Of the self-referential.

FANTASTIC PRAYERS

O du Metallvogel meine Seele

RICHARD HUELSENBECK
Phantastische Gebete

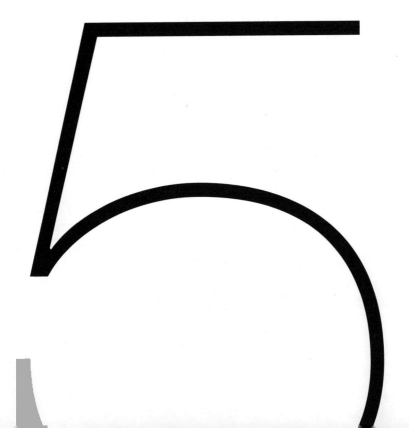

The following "prayers" are not supplications but offerings to Negation, hence, to the possibility of language (which, as a total system, can never be inhabited by consciousness). The title is taken from the Dada poem-cycle Phantastische Gebete *by Richard Huelsenbeck, first published in Zürich in 1916.*

I

Signs of the flock returning.
—flicker
    at the standstill of certainty.

Cavern where the words were stained.

Entrance
    the imperative
    to pour this trace.

Chalice, couch.
Anthill, whore.

Dust, desire
    is the rapturous study of distance.

[*blasts*]

MOUND TO SOUND: DER MUND.

MINED
MIND
MOANED.

MOANED
MONAD.

OPEN STOPS. OPEN STOPS.

CHORD ECHO CORD.
UNMANNED.

GRAND GROUND UNDER.

II

The breast tenebrous. Shape alone
& pale relation.

    Heaven, mineral
    voids music.

Avenue whose purpose is to be repaired.
        —the branching
Thought to be broken.

Held startlement, only
        a disturbed bird, "city without a center."

The earthly chapter a charred heap.

[blasts]

DARK MARKER
THE MAKER.

NEVER THE NERVE
OF ARRIVAL.

NERVE
TO CURVE TO CARVE.

PARED OBJECT TO COME
COMPARED TO SUBJECT.

UNSOWN, UNSEWN, THE SKY'S OWN
SKIN, WHOSE BLUES
END? BLEND? IN HIGH INVISIBILITY.

III

The sound of a trumpet decays
Like an animal.

A trail leads back to the loud revelation.

Earth's black table tilts below time.

Schmerz ist der Grundton der Natur.
No shimmering to agree with itself.

Later
        violins to translate violence.
        The massed mountains audience.
That
        thing think thing, sound signed deaf.

[blasts]

INHABITED ABANDON.
WEST OF THE WEST

WELLED SILENCES.
THE SUN'S UNDONE, UNDYING EDDIES.

STRUM—DER STURM

WHIRLED TO DRAIN FROM
THIS
FRAUGHT AIR OR ERROR—DRUM.

JOY TO—FREED
BEAUTY FROM AGENCY.
FREUDE.

IV

Held startlement, a handful of water.

Likelihood of fault, star, cloud.

Erasure shines like Heraclitus.
—once
Living, what lovers will turn to letters—

Leaves are the eyes that carry correspondences.

As "clasp" ends in a whisper.

Unclose.

Unclose.

[blasts]

THING, NAILED.
THOUGHT, KNELLED.

KNELLS.

TELLS, TOLLS, ROLLS
LAMPLESS.
O OUTERMOST PLANET.

PLUTONIAN SUN
OR CORRODED CODE.

RING OF THOUGHT
ALMOST THING.

∨

The motion of all that is
Missing, massing here.

Before
  the red book of the unwritten body.

Field of the failed aleph, a laugh after
    life.
  Full of the familiar foreign O.

Thus prayer is poured out of empty prose.

In harmony a harm—
    the one called but not named. To scatter
  Asking—answering swerve of recursive matter.

[*blasts*]

INVIOLATE
VOLUME.

TREMBLING GLOBE

OF BLOWN GLASS.

ENTRANCE TO TRACE.

ALIGHTED, ELIDED
ALL
LIGHTED THOUGHT.

ALL COUNTER
TO THE CUMULATIVE.

VI *after Celan*

Engführung—forced into the narrows.

As driven as drawn there—who
Reduces to whom.

Aghast, against—
The paradox a fixity not an opening.

Akt mit Rauchseele. Umnachtet. Owl's flight
Under storied stones, the fled immensities.

Ho, ho-
  sianna.
   How, without motive, to display this
Mind of howling splendor?

[*blasts*]

BELL, CRUCIBLE, ECHO.

BECKON, BEACON, BECOME

COMBER TO CAVE, TO
WAVE.

STRAYED AS STRAIGHTENING.

BOOK, SUN, BEAK.

SEEK BY CAUL, CALL
CROW.

BELL, CRUCIBLE, ECHO.

VII

Rocks in a constellation, the infant Sun.

A line extending to—
The "most beautiful" is not meaning.

    —the new world
Entered as ending, the widening fact.

To follow directionless
The rays. A verb reverberant in the tense of time.

From the fragment *cosm* arrive at *chasm.*
From the name of the guest arrive at ghost.

Rays to rise as random O, as dome.

[*blasts*]

ONE
ORBIC NUMBER, OF

COAL, OF COWL, OF CALL.

SMOKE-ENGENDERED.
AIR-SMITTEN

IMAGE, RED
ROOD.

OF
VELOCITIES, THE UNMOTIVATED
IDEA.
THE DERELICT DOLL.

VIII

Only exits exist.

Dear ruler: Every symmetry
Has its axis, as every tree its axe.

—all falls to the exchange of equals.

This cut connects this
        but cannot differ from itself
As a chambered solid, sky or skull.

        Take speechless
        over inspirited, the referent
        that quits its task.
Let question answer, or revolution.

[blasts]

BURN DOWN BEING

BUT DO NOT ABOLISH SHADOW.
SHADOW

REMAINS NECESSARY TO THE BODY
THAT HIDES ITS SOURCE.

IF NOT THE BODY, THEN THE BED.
IF NOT THE BOUNDARY, THEN THE PRECIPICE

OF THE PRIOR MOMENT
INFINITE IN FALLING AWAY.

HELD, HEROIC: EARTH'S SHADOW-HALF.

IX

Noon, noun, no
      known—
No one.

Noon hides nothing.

Now, whose nulling arrival needs one
      isonomic insomniac voice—

Now rings this dispersal that is spoken.

Noon reverses its name to resurrect sound.
Noon pours toward its opposite, trace over trance.

Zero opens (a zero-rose) sideways in time.

[*blasts*]

NOON.
NOUN.
NO
KNOWN, NO ONE.

NOON HIDES NOTHING.

NOW'S NULLING
SOUND.
NOW SOUND.

NOON
NOON

ZERO.

X

Earth was forged—a serpentine line.
Of necessity, a thread thrown down.

So signature was made to imitate chance.

Thus, the "edge of the world"
Appeared
      neither as wall nor as picture.

Is the amphitheater
Rotational to ruin?

Let this flesh, in a flash, become
Mathematical sand.
Amen.

[blasts]

BLESSED ABLEST
SIGN.
WINNOWED WINDOWED
SCENE.

ACCUSATIVE TO CANCEL.
NOMINATIVE TO CONSOLE.

THE DENSE TO DANCE, ENSOULED
SOLID.

OF OFFER, OF
FEAR, OF FIRE. GIVE
A GENITIVE LANGUAGE, OR FUROR.
AMEN.

Andrew Joron was born in San Antonio, Texas, in 1955 and grew up in Stuttgart, Germany; Lowell, Massachusetts; and Missoula, Montana. He attended the University of California at Berkeley, where he majored in history and philosophy of science. After a decade and a half spent writing science-fiction poetry, culminating in his volume *Science Fiction* (Pantograph Press, 1992), he turned to a more philosophical mode of speculative lyric. This work has been collected in *The Removes* (Hard Press, 1999) and in the present volume. He is also the translator, from the German, of the Marxist-Utopian philosopher Ernst Bloch's *Literary Essays* (Stanford University Press, 1998), and of the surrealist Richard Anders's aphorisms and prose poems. Andrew Joron lives in Berkeley, where he works as a freelance bibliographer and indexer.